THE MARINE
PHOTOGRAPHY
of PETER BARLOW

12-meter sloop Columbia behind a swell off Newport.

THE MARINE PHOTOGRAPHY of PETER BARLOW

MOTOR BOATING & SAILING BOOKS
NEW YORK, N. Y.

Designer: Peter Barlow

Editor: John R. Whiting

Copyright © by The Hearst Corporation
959 Fifth Avenue, New York, N.Y. 10019
Library of Congress catalog card number: 72-89439
ISBN   0-910990-14-X

Printed for Motor Boating & Sailing Books
by Vinmar Lithographing Company, Timonium, Maryland

To
DORRIE

It doesn't seem to matter how
the light shines on her

Introduction

THERE WAS no boating in my family. My father came from a farm in Texas and said the only water he knew was the watering tank for cattle where he sometimes swam. My mother lived near the Potomac River and enjoyed rowing in her early childhood, just before moving to Illinois. My older brother had some brief interest in boats but apparently it was given no encouragement. And while our home in Westport, Connecticut was only a few miles from Long Island Sound, I was 22 before I was ever aboard a sailboat.

I grew up among artists. My father began doing cartoons for *The New Yorker* when the magazine started and has been with them ever since. My mother's art career was at a peak in the late 1920s and 30s. She painted pictures of children for illustrations and advertising. In those days before photography dominated advertisements, paintings of babies were widely used to sell soap and other products. One of her drawings, for a manufacturer of baby foods, became a world famous trademark—the Gerber baby.

With art as the family profession it was no surprise that I drew pictures from a very early age—mostly of cars. If boating was unknown to us, photography was known as something not to be taken very seriously. It was fun to make snapshots but I always had the feeling that it was sort of an inadequate and mechanical way of doing what artists did better. Besides, I was told, photography was taking work away from artists. Dad would often see a photo he liked that had some unusual, moody character about it but he would praise it in a way to suggest that somehow it must have been an accident. He liked some of the earliest photographs and I had the impression that the craft had gone downhill ever since. But my mother used photography in her later work when she began painting portraits of children. She would make a movie of a child and then project it into a hatbox next to her easel. She could stop the movie on any frame and felt this was the best way to study a natural expression, since children tend to freeze up for still photos and don't like to hold a pose for a painter. Mother did pretty well with her movies even though she said she didn't know much about taking them, which was true.

The first camera I owned was called a Univex. My parents bought it for me when I was six and it cost 19 cents at Liggett's. I took the usual pictures of family and friends in the backyard squinting into the sun. Then one day we were driving past an airport in Danbury and there parked on the ground was an airplane I wanted to photograph. I went up close to it and took a picture, head-on. When the picture came back from the drugstore I was very pleased and told myself it was especially good because few people ever got that close to an airplane.

At the age of ten I was taking pictures of animals with another camera called a Baby Brownie Special. There was a squirrel that used to come to our door for walnuts. He would climb on the windowsill and rattle the doorknob with his paw—a signal for me to open the door and hand him a nut on a wooden spoon. One day I took a photograph of him through the window while he was waiting there for his walnut. I liked that picture and it seemed to prove that I was closer to a squirrel than most people get.

At about this time there was a lady in our neighborhood who had a darkroom. She invited me to bring over some negatives and said she would show me how enlargements are made. I had never given a thought to how pictures were printed and so it came as quite a surprise in her darkroom to see her putting this paper into trays of liquid. The idea of paper in water seemed incredible. But seeing the picture image come up in the developer was fascinating—this is one of those moments of commitment for photographers-to-be. Interesting as it was, I was really more interested in just having the enlargements and instead of asking her to show me more about print-making, I found myself simply asking her to make enlargements for me. And she did, quite briefly.

In the next few years I became more involved with creative efforts of other people and started collecting things—stamps, coins, telephone pole insulators, foreign handicrafts, wood carvings, pottery and metal objects. All of these had in common some element of design that appealed to me. My tastes improved with age and by the mid-teens I was picking up Siamese buddhas and Asian antiques. Such things were scarce then and not much in demand and dealers who had them didn't know anything about them. I used to mow lawns for spending money and then go to New York City to browse through curio shops. With an end to World War II and the entry of the United States into the life of Asia, objects from that part of the world became fashionable, and expensive, and I was looking in other directions.

Modern art from Vincent Van Gogh to Salvador Dali was the next interest, followed by trumpet-playing in jazz groups. Painting became a serious endeavor and it seemed likely that this would be my profession. I was also taking photographs again and although darkroom work had no appeal, I studied negatives very carefully and would send them to mail-order photo finishers with elaborate instructions for small enlargements. Some of these firms did quite good work. The photos were not end products in themselves but they gave me ideas for paintings. After high school I went briefly to the Art Students League in New York. The school was crowded with returning veterans and the instructors gave little time to each student so I decided instead to rent a small place to work on my own, adding some income by making picture frames and painting signs. Lettering was an instinctive ability inherited from my mother but I wasn't very fast at it. However I was selling a reasonable number of paintings. The subjects included jazz impressions and portraits of musicians, which were based on my photographs. There were also many scenes of architecture in some form, more often than I ever realized.

With no boating in my life up to this time there should have been some spectacular sight or experience to bring about the nearly total involvement with boats that followed. Nothing so dramatic occurred. One summer day I was walking along Compo Beach in Westport looking out past the bathers at some sailboats far in the distance. It was a familiar view but this was probably the first time I had given any thought to sailboats. Actually the sailboats were only a part of a total mood. The sky and water seemed remarkably open, almost three-dimensional, as if there were huge segments of blue space. This feeling of space was intriguing and I began thinking about a new series of paintings in which distance, especially movement through distance, would be a dominant interest. The idea of space was not really new. I never liked crowds or being cramped and objects always looked better with enough room around them. It was fun to walk through the woods but the best part was coming out into a clearing. A single tree in a field was always more interesting than a forest. My paintings and photographs had usually been of single subjects or sometimes pairs. And now, nothing was quite so ideally symbolic of the feeling of space—and air and light—as a sailboat.

Aside from that, there was practically nothing I knew about sailboats and for the rest of the season I studied boats and took photos of them coming in and out of harbors and also made pictures of anchors, docks, seaweed—anything of marine interest that could be seen from the shore. Most of all I wanted to go out in a sailboat. Knowing no owners of boats, I put up a small notice in several yacht clubs saying something like "young photographer wishes to come aboard sailing boat of any kind to take compositional pictures of sails and rigging. . . ." One of my early observations about boat owners was that they don't invite strangers to go sailing with them. (A few years later I would also notice, conversely, that boat owners are often desperate for sailing companions.) Late in the season a distant relative invited me for a ride in his outboard motorboat. We went out early on a Sunday morning and soon discovered a ketch name *Freya*. She was a gaff-rigged boat designed by William Atkin and only about 32 feet but she looked to me like a great historic sailing vessel coming out of the mist. We came up very close to her and I took several pictures and even wondered if many people got this close to a sailing boat. She was doing all of two knots at the time. It occurred to me later that if I could locate the owner and give him some prints he might invite me to sail in this great boat.

Mr. George Richards, Vice Commodore of the Cruising Club of America and owner of *Freya*, was having his dinner when I knocked on the door of his house, but he paused long enough to thank me for the pictures and reach for some money which I declined. There was no invitation but in the brief conversation about boats and pictures I gathered that a man who sails doesn't get to see his own boat sailing. I also made a mental note that boat owners will pay for photographs.

In the next two years—exploring my new interest—I did many paintings of boats, continued taking photos, taught myself to print photographs, went sailing frequently with a new friend who owned a 15-foot Bullseye sloop, and bought my first "good" camera—a Rolleicord. Then I acquired my first boat —an old Cape Cod knockabout sloop, 16 feet long and with it, an outboard motor. The plan was to use the motor when taking pictures and sail the rest of the time. It worked for a while but then every time I raised the sails there would be some fine vessel in the distance that had to be photographed so I would lower the sails and motor on out for more pictures. And often it took a long time since this boat was not very fast under sail or power.

However I photographed many boats from it and found owners anxious to buy my pictures which were sent to them on approval. Soon it was clear that a fast motorboat was essential for marine photography and that sailing, for the most part, would have to be sacrificed. The local harbormaster owned a small inboard launch that at one time had been a Chris Craft speedboat, but with the addition of a shelter cabin looked very different. When Capt. Tooker decided to part with her, I switched to power. The new boat was quite an advance in mobility and required different techniques for picture-taking.

Garry Moore, of television, owned a yawl named *Redwing* which I had photographed once before from my sailboat. I encountered *Redwing* again in the motorboat in a better wind and attempted to take photographs of her by aiming the camera out the window while running my boat at the same time. The eventual prints seemed pretty good but Mr. Moore, on receiving them, wrote back that he was disappointed. There was a slack in the genoa and he didn't think the pictures came off as well as the first ones with just the working sails. Mr. Moore had not been aboard his boat when I took the earlier pictures and in his letter he added this paragraph:

> "It is probably an illusion, but in the first pictures you seem to have shot from a lower angle—which had the happy effect of making the hull loom larger against the horizon, as tho your original boat had less freeboard. Or perhaps it's the very fact that in the first pictures the waterline of *Redwing* very nearly coincides with the horizon."

That observation proved to be significant because in fact I had been taking photographs from a lower angle in my sailboat, but without knowing that it was in any way unusual. I used to sit in the stern of the boat while operating the outboard and just for sheer convenience the way to take pictures was to hold the camera over the side of the boat (the twin-lens reflex camera is the type one looks down into). The boat didn't have much freeboard so the camera was little more than an inch from the water. Looking over some of my previous pictures I realized that this low angle effect was pleasing and contributed to the feeling of space that I liked. Most people see a sailboat from a level at which the horizon comes between the deck and the boom. This is an area that is already crowded and it makes an unfortunate place to divide a picture. By lowering the camera a few feet the horizon is put close to the waterline and the perspective and lines of the hull are greatly enhanced. And so with my motorboat I learned a shooting technique of hanging over the side or out the window to get low-angle views. It became a natural routine after a while although it must have looked strange. Boat owners would often won-

Brandaris

der what I was doing: Some thought I was picking up lobster pots or fishing. "How are they biting?" was a frequent greeting and probably more than one thought I was ill. There was one particular disadvantage to the low angle—it never made the water look as rough as it really was. But this happens in all boating photography—anyone who takes pictures on the water may come back telling about seven-foot waves and then find that the pictures don't look anything like that. The low angle view also requires shooting at close range with normal lenses since any view from a distance reduces the angle upward. This type of picture was my trademark for a long time but now with other lenses and cameras, it is only one of several approaches. Garry Moore's comment had started me thinking about style. Having a fast motorboat enabled me to cover a larger area of Long Island Sound and might have resulted in a near mass production of photographs or even the possibility of "running out of boats." Instead, with a choice of boats, I became selective.

It used to be a popular idea that beauty in the lines of a boat was a natural quality of one that performed well. William Fife, the Scottish designer who created *Cotton Blossom IV* is credited with saying, "the ship that looks right, is right." This was certainly true of *Cotton Blossom* but the statement doesn't always hold up. Today it's even naive since there are so many boats of less than attractive lines that are very successful. Some are designed to get the best rating for racing and some are built from the inside out with emphasis on interior space and comfort—true especially of powerboats. However, any craft that is designed to move through or over water inevitably has some aesthetic qualities about it. The "ship that looks right" is most likely to be the one that interests me.

Once I spent two days on a small island taking photographs of rocks and branches and anything that seemed interesting. It was an exercise to see how many different views could be found within the limits of a given area. Photographing boats is not so different. The sea is presented with its own set of limitations, which change—the wind, light, tides, and currents—and the photographer learns to work within these conditions using them to best advantage whenever possible. How the boats appear and how well the crews sail them may also be called a limitation because the photographer doesn't usually place the boats—he finds them there, as in a race.

I have two approaches to marine photography and they overlap to some degree. The first is to show a boat at its best, as the creation the designer wants to see, and as I want to see in terms of the play of light and shade on the various shapes. Such pictures might be called "portraits" but that's not a seaworthy word and suggests something still and posed and merely representational. A boat is almost a living thing and its picture ought to breathe a little or convey some kind of atmosphere. Pictures in this category are the hardest to make mainly because they involve conditions beyond the photographer's control. Wind and light directions must be in the right alignment to produce the desired effect. Most of the time they are not.

My second approach to marine photography takes in everything else: pictures that show the nature of boating, racing situations, activities around boats and harbors and a lot of little sights on the fringes of boating that have some special appeal to me. In this approach there is no sole intention of seeing boats looking well—the pictures may even be quite unflattering but some element of interest provides the reason for taking them. It's an area for observing and reporting. I think of myself more as an observer than a reporter. Many of the things I notice are not especially good reporting in the news sense. Some of the pictures may have news value but I see them only as pictures.

A sailboat looks best from her leeward side, the side to which she is heeling (for some reason this point confuses people and I have to emphasize "leeward side, not looking to leeward"). The most attractive lighting occurs when the boat is headed in nearly the direction of the sun, or perhaps with the sun slightly more to leeward. The forward parts of the sails are in full light and taper off into shadow giving a fullness to the sails and perhaps a pleasing shadow of the jib or rigging across the mainsail (see *Silver Night*, page 40). Sometimes there will also be a backlighted area beyond the shadow in the lower, after section of the sails. With this lighting a series of views can be taken from different angles on the leeward side, from nearly head-on to a stern quarter view. It is part of my attitude about boat pictures to think of them in a sequence rather than one overall view. A boat has many facets and they all should be observed. However, each boat has a few preferred angles and perhaps one to be avoided, such as an overly large stern. I tend to like off the bow views but a large genoa may obscure everything else from this angle. A few boats look well only in full broadside views while there are others that may look longer and more graceful from off the bow than they really are. Telephoto lenses destroy any illusion such as that and generally it is undesirable to use a telephoto lens in a picture of an individual boat, although they are effective for groups or racing scenes.

Views of a sailboat from the windward side are usually chosen by manufacturers of bottom paint. A broadside view from this side produces far too much foreshortening of the mast if the boat is heeling. However there is considerable appeal in an off-the-bow, windward view (*Rosa II*, page 61) or a

quarter view of a schooner or other vessel with an unusual amount of rigging (*St. Lawrence II*, page 76).

The conditions for photographing boats are seldom ideal, especially on Long Island Sound. The wind there comes from all directions, usually on the light side but sometimes very gusty. The best wind velocity for pictures is between 15 and 25 knots, or higher if the aim is to show wild action. Many boats will reef down in higher winds which of course reduces the action and others may look badly if they are having difficulty. On several occasions I have watched boats of the Star class racing in very gusty winds. A Star skipper often must let his sails luff frantically to keep from breaking the mast. This may be a fact of life to be reported photographically, but a luffing sail stopped by the camera in mid-luff is not very attractive. And a sail luffing unnecessarily in a lesser wind is a flaw. Surprisingly, most of the boats I see are not suited for being photographed at the time, either because the wind and light are not right or because something doesn't look quite right—a line over the side, a sail not properly set, or many other things.

Boating photography is often done "by appointment" especially for advertising pictures. There are advantages and disadvantages to this. Everything can be done to make the boat presentable but the weather is still an unknown factor. And manufacturers generally don't want much action in their pictures—a boat that's heeling over apparently scares away customers. The most satisfying marine photographs are almost always made when the photographer is out on his own, on a proper day, shooting the best performing or most interesting boats he can find. I keep a list of owners and clients who ask to have pictures taken at such times, particularly when they have their racing crews.

The water is also shared by powerboats. If the sounds and smells of engines make their owners less able to savor the sea, they are at least very happy to be there. Designers of sailboats also create powerboats so it is appropriate for a marine photographer to take pictures of these boats as well, especially on calmer days when sailing is uninviting. Powerboats are less of a problem to photograph and are not dependent on wind of course, but there is almost always something wrong with their appearance: a dirt streak running down the hull, a dinghy heaped on the deck, or that great badge of mindless boating—the fender flopping against the hull as the boat goes merrily along. A bit nobler in my view are the working boats that travel the Sound—tugs, fishing boats, tankers and freighters. I have a visual curiosity about anything that is designed to move on the water and also those things that don't move—lighthouses, buoys, and islands.

Coming back to the "ship that looks right," my own preferences in boats

Manisses

are not easily defined but always have a visual basis. I like to see a balanced rig and hull, cabins or other structures in good relative proportions, attractive angles, and curves that have a proper continuity in their flow. Actually, what I would like to see sailing up Long Island Sound is a great Arab dhow —all the qualities just mentioned in a different combination. But if the Sound were full of dhows I would then be interested in only the unique ones.

I like boats that have several sails simply because they offer more to look at, more possibilities for lighting and patterns. Sails and rigging are the primary invitations. Hulls may become equally important if they have distinctive shapes but I tend to notice less about hulls in general than about sail plans. Boats with many sails are frequently older types and this explains my fondness for old and traditional vessels more than any special reverence for tradition. I've always liked schooners. In addition to carrying a number of sails the schooner has a look of stately momentum that comes from having the tallest and largest sail aft. Some older cutters also have this look. Yawls and ketches, whether old or new, can carry four or five sails and I will often seek them out in a sailing fleet in preference to sloops. There are just as many interesting sloops as other types, probably more, but there are so many sloops— and so many all the same or similar—that the rig is the one that interests me least. I think of sloops as basic boats with all others as elaborations—much as when I was a child choosing ice cream, vanilla was plain and everything else was a flavor. Sloops, I can't help thinking, are plain. Still, if I have a sailboat again it will be a sloop, or maybe a small cutter. I might name it *Vanilla*.

The performance of a boat does not concern me as a photographer unless it relates to the picture, but in a personal sense some amount of efficiency is expected. I do have a regard for the relation of appearance to function in any effort and as much disdain for a good looking design that functions poorly as for an unattractive design whether it works or not. While it is intellectually satifying to know that a boat I like is, in fact, a "good" boat or even a classic of its kind, I also feel free to enjoy a lumbering, romantic ark if it appeals to me. Any number of interesting elements or circumstances may outweigh a vessel's deficiency although it's better if it does reasonably well at something.

Another concern is craftsmanship. Quality construction, particularly in minute details, may not always be apparent in an overall view of a boat but it should be there for close inspection—and I do like looking closely at things. This is also a reason for liking traditional boats—many of the original ones have extraordinary workmanship. Craftsmanship is most often associated with fine wood work, not surprisingly after centuries of wooden boats. Recognizing

Kestrel

Super Sprites

that heritage, one fiberglass boat builder advertises "simulated plank seams"—curious, since seams were usually well concealed on yachts of wood.

Fiberglass has had a large impact on the appearance of boats and the material allows many kinds of shapes that could not be done in wood, especially in the combination of molded decks and cabins. While many of the early fiberglass boats were unattractive—their finishes deteriorated and they were devoid of wood since that conflicted with the original goal of no maintainance—better designs and building techniques and the eventual recognition of the logic of fiberglass as a hull material have made its use nearly universal. There is still a tendency for many of the boats to have a boring sameness in their design but more of them are being built with wood trim, teak decks, and wood cabins and interiors. The best of these are impressively good looking and in a few cases it is even hard to tell at a glance if the hulls really are fiberglass. I like seeing several surfaces with different tones and textures. Such separations improve the lines of a boat whereas one that has the same unrelieved color over the entire hull, deck and cabin looks more like a cake of soap. But sometimes the added trim is a pretty shallow effort—on close examination the teak deck may be revealed as some kind of rubber matting glued in place. Fakery and illusion have always been part of the American culture but somehow there is more appeal for me in the false front of an old western saloon than in a cake of soap with a rubber teak mat.

Along with the use of fiberglass as a factor in the appearance of boats is the designing of one category of them according to rating formulas for racing. The effect of this requires some explanation.

As experienced racers know, boats of different sizes and shapes require a handicapping system in order to compete together fairly, in contrast to one-design boats which race only with others of the same design. The usual method is to give a boat a certain time allowance which is subtracted after the race from her "elapsed time" over the course, leaving a "corrected time." It is the corrected time that counts in the final results even though the actual order of boats crossing the finish line may be quite different. The size of a boat's time allowance is determined by her "rating," a figure that comes out of a complex formula based on a number of measurements of the boat—her overall length, waterline length, beam, draft, sail area and other considerations. The rating formula is known as the "rule" and there have been several different rules in use with continuing efforts to improve, change or unify them.

A low rating is desirable to get a large time allowance and a resulting competitive advantage. In designing a winning boat the goal is not pure speed but rather the best possible relationship between speed and rating, since elements that contribute to the fastest speed might produce a high rating and a losing boat. Rating rules favor certain features of a boat and give penalties to others. Large mainsails have been penalized for some years, so racing boats have had relatively small mains and huge overlapping genoa jibs. The current preference is for taller but very narrow mainsails along with the large fore-triangle areas favored by ratings. Other visible characteristics have included shallow, tubby hulls, small reverse sheer transoms and a trend to sloops over other rigs. Designing a boat according to a rule or to circumvent the rule often leads to artificial appearance concepts and rampant imitation follows whenever one good gimmick is found. As a result, a system that in theory was intended to measure the potential of diverse boats so they could compete together has come to dominate yacht design and rule out much of the diversity.

These boats have generally been known as racer-cruisers. Presumably they might compete in the 200-mile Block Island Race but would also have the comforts and accommodations for families to cruise leisurely along the coast. However, offshore racing has become so specialized that many of the qualities of good cruising have been sacrificed to produce more competitive boats. Comfort may be expendable—a wet, bumpy ride is tolerable when you're out to win, ease of handling is not too important with a large crew and those winches, and beauty is said to be a performance that brings in silverware. Still, there are a number of good looking racing boats. There could be more or fewer in another cycle of rule changes.

The majority of sailors do not race. They enjoy the water as they choose, which may be day-sailing, or if their boats are suitably designed, cruising for longer distances on open water. While many of these boats have benefitted from the technology brought about by racing, it is unnecessary for them to be influenced by some of the requirements of racing or by those limitations imposed by measurement rules (though many cruisers are). Cruising boats are designed more for a high average of performance than for such specific needs as getting to a windward mark or sailing in one particular kind of air. They are more likely to follow basic principles of design suitable for sea conditions that remain unchanged. Beauty in these boats is a requisite for the cruising experience.

Beauty is also personal and subjective, a variable that tends to be established in terms of familiarity—the "way boats ought to look." It is worth noting that a few of the forms that now seem traditional were thought to be pretty unorthodox, if not plain ugly, when first introduced—certain bow shapes, for example.

Designers of cruising boats have a considerable latitude in developing their

concepts of beauty. There are occasions however when sales promotion demands the utmost accommodations in a given hull length and in some cases the exterior appearance cannot hide the accomplishment. Such a boat may still look all right if the design is in harmony with itself—extreme boats are frequently very interesting. But a boat with extreme over-rigging will be more interesting than a short one sleeping eight.

For pictures, cruising boats may not show as much action as the lighter racing boats or have the large inventories of sails. Aside from that, they are boats that I like. Many are also racers from another day.

There is one final twist in my consideration of a boat. While I see many interesting and attractive vessels that could be very promising subjects, my appreciation is not quite committed until after I have taken pictures. And even then, my estimation of the boat is affected by the photographic quality or satisfaction of each picture. That may seem remote to most sailors, but in my way of boating involvement there is little separation between boats and pictures.

The pictures originally were to be paintings, not photographs. Oddly, it was the interest in boats that turned me away from being a painter. Texture effects were becoming something of an obsession and I found increasing difficulty in producing any sense of what boats were suggesting. At the same time the need to sell paintings was present and I didn't like doing the sort of literal renditions that yachtsmen buy. While my early boat photographs were taken with the intention of building a file of reference material for future paintings, owners of boats who saw me with my camera were more immediately interested in buying the photographs—a fact that was too convenient to ignore. I no longer paint, except in some limited design areas, but painting is still a subject of interest.

Marine art was a more recognized endeavor when sailing ships were essential to American life. In the 1800s there were such noted ship painters as Robert Salmon, James E. Buttersworth and Fitz Hugh Lane. At present, with yachts only as important as luxury, the speciality of painting them is far removed from all but lovers of boats. Sadly, the limitation seems to be in a preoccupation with subject matter. Painters who have as much feeling for their medium as they do for boats rarely confine themselves to the one subject.

There are a great many artists of different periods and styles whose works have been significant to me. Three can be mentioned here for the way they have handled boat themes.

Albert Pinkham Ryder (1847–1917) painted moonlight boats and turbulent seas that were images from his mind, though perhaps with memories of his early life in New Bedford as well. If he had a detailed knowledge of boats it never interfered with the bold, simplified shapes that he often distorted for the rhythm of his compositions. He worked with many layers of pigments and glazes to produce rich surface effects, although his lack of concern for the drying properties of these mediums caused most of his paintings to crack and discolor. Nonetheless, he is considered the most original and imaginative American artist of his time.

William Thon is a contemporary painter with an evident appreciation for boats. He frequently uses shapes of hulls in partially abstracted planes, combining them with subtleties of texture and lighting. He paints similar effects with architecture and trees—subjects that also appeal to me.

Andrew Wyeth is well known to most everyone. He has done relatively few paintings with boat themes but there is a distinct sense of air and breeze in many of his scenes and for me, a feeling of water nearby. His exquisite technique, real but not photographic, is the kind that is compatible with the likeness of a ship. A New England schooner would be fine.

Characteristics of photography had some early effects on me, even if overshadowed by other influences. I can remember in my childhood the rotogravure section of the Sunday papers where the pictures were printed in brown ink in a high quality of reproduction, perhaps my first notice that printing quality made a difference. And I recall being absorbed with the pictures in several volumes of a German camera annual at a friend's house. Photographs have impressed me for various reasons but I have had little acquaintance with professional photographers or knowledge of their attitudes about the medium. There was one exception.

Kurt Smith was a photographer and technician who worked at Reed's Camera Shop. He had an idea that I would do more with photography than seemed likely at the time. Rather than sell me the hobby-style of photo enlarger I was considering, he let me borrow his own superior enlarger, knowing the encouragement that good equipment would give. We became friends and he was a technical consultant whenever I was stuck with a problem. Kurt never found much success except in helping people, but he was eager and imaginative and enjoyed doing things like playing his trumpet in a cemetery. According to his moods he would seem Chinese, Spanish or Near Eastern, though today he would more proudly be black. Yesterday's world confined him to a mental hospital in Newtown, Conn.

Working for publications has been an important experience. For the past ten years I have been doing monthly photographic essays for *Soundings*, a boating newspaper put out by an energetic, fun-loving group of friends.

While they have left me fairly free to plan these pages, the association has given me a much wider outlook in the range of editorial coverage and for the uses of pictures in general. Most of the photographs in this book were first printed in *Soundings*. My work has also appeared in *Motor Boating & Sailing* and other boating magazines.

Photography was not a conscious choice for a profession. I used to say that taking pictures of boats represented more of an interest in boats than in photos. That is no longer true. The medium has finally come to be a purpose in its own right and the ideas I once transposed from snapshots into paintings are now more effectively shown in photographs.

Photography is a means of looking at things and remembering them. It is far more immediate than painting and more suited to sequences of views or variations and a rapid accumulation of images. I like this aspect and much of my satisfaction comes from seeing pictures in pairs or groups that "work" together, showing some relationship—a similarity or contrast, a pattern or point of view. While paintings and photographs share some elements of pictorial harmony, they have many different characteristics and purposes and I prefer to emphasize the differences. Photography may be an art form in some of its applications but it ought to be its own form, free from such "arty" misreadings as printing pictures on canvas textures or giving them titles. The field of cinema can be described as a complete art form but I wonder if a single photograph of a tree should be any more a work of art than the tree. More important than the question of art is the fact that photography is a language of sorts—a visual dialogue to convey observations or elicit responses.

If the medium is a creative expression for me, it is not a native language in some of its technical and chemical processes. However this is the area of its individuality. Over the years I have realized the importance of processing and how much of a picture's effectiveness depends on a control of personal taste in the chemistry. And knowing exactly what I want, it is nearly inconceivable to have someone else make my prints. It's a nice thought though because I'm not really fond of working in the darkroom.

Knowing what I want is only an awareness at each moment—the unpredictable nature of picture-taking is one of the things that makes it inviting. However after twenty years, boating has become predictable. I am accustomed to the situations, to the wind and light combinations, and knowing what to expect leaves a little less adventure. And the present boats are also familiar. I still want to see dhows and feluccas, junks, Thames barges and sail training ships. One of my unfulfilled projects has been to produce a photographic collection of vanishing types around the world. But there are other facets of boating and boat photography to explore and my enthusiasm is encouraged by those few new vessels like *Bill of Rights* (pages 82–83), or Atkin designs of about 30 feet, or lovely little rowing boats that people build in their basements.

At the same time, a better feeling for the medium of photography stimulates curiosity in a variety of subject matter. Architecture, my long unconscious interest, is now a photographic hobby. It is concerned mainly with exterior forms in light and shade, inevitably making a preference for unusual structures (a parallel to boats?). Other subjects include trees, bridges, different kinds of transportation and amusement park rides. Not surprisingly, I have also become attracted to many things that relate to children—my own little girl, who is now four, is a new focus in my life. It doesn't seem to matter how the light shines on her.

Peter Barlow
Westport, Connecticut
May, 1973

THE MARINE
PHOTOGRAPHY
of PETER BARLOW

A Look at the Water

Most people like water. Many will live nearby or visit even if they never venture on it. Rivers, ponds, brooks and distant views of the sea are all memorable in our lives. Water is the basic element of marine photography—perhaps one could photograph nothing else since the nature of the sea is just as variable as boats and sailors.

Most sailors will look at the water before setting forth.

Water is usually seen in some degree of motion. The still camera has a unique ability to stop this movement for a view that reveals the meaty texture of a wave or the ghostliness of ripples.

Race Rock Light near Fishers Island.

LIGHTS

Lighthouses are historic structures, some dating to the late 1700s, and they are friends to most sailors. But they are becoming obsolete. Gradually they are being abandoned or demolished and replaced by skeletal towers with automated equipment. However, many citizens—sailors or not—take a community pride in their nearby lighthouses and rally to preserve those that are threatened. Bell and light buoys and other navigational aids are often decorative and a sort of punctuation along the way. They are not as affectionately regarded as lighthouses even though the image of a bell buoy is a symbol common to all users of the water.

"The Spider" at Annapolis.

No. 24 is a standard 9 x 32 bell and light buoy—9 feet is the diameter, 32 is the length (17½ feet above water and 14½ below). The underwater portion includes a balancing tube and counterweight.

A view inside the French-made Fresnel lens of Eatons Neck Light. Augustin Fresnel (1788–1827) revolutionized lighthouse illumination using his compound lenses instead of the earlier mirror system.

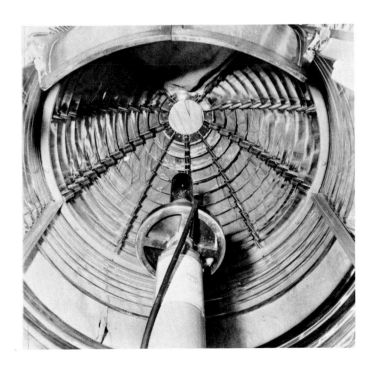

Lighthouses are not often notable examples of construction but certain ones are quite distinctive. Some might be included in the small category of round or octagonal buildings that appears in every age of American architecture. Thomas Point Shoal Light is six sided. This is one of the screw-pile lighthouses of the Chesapeake (piles somewhat auger-shaped and driven into the ground). Southeast Light at Block Island is a handsome brick structure built in 1873 and stands near 150 foot cliffs overlooking the Atlantic Ocean. The shore sites of lighthouses, having been picked in earlier ages of real estate, are invariably some of the most desirable locations along the coast.

Greens Ledge Light, long maintained by a three man crew, was slated for destruction in 1971 but protests led the Coast Guard to incorporate their new devices into the existing structure.

Bell and Light No. 24 in haze. This is an earlier buoy that burns compressed acetylene gas and requires a larger lamp than the present battery-operated light.

RIGS & TYPES

A long time ago I met an artist who made a living by painting portraits of horses. I found it unusual that anyone could work in such a narrow specialty, but the most amazing thing was to learn that horses looked different enough that their portraits could be painted. It is curious that we seldom think of differences in areas that are unfamiliar. Some people will even proclaim this inability with the dismissal, "if you've seen one, you've seen them all."

Unlike horses however, the first thing I noticed about boats was their differences—they came in all sorts of shapes and even when the shapes were the same, the proportions and size changed. It was the shapes of boats that interested me most, and probably still is. I quickly learned to identify these according to rig—sloop, cutter, ketch, etc. Then came the discovery that in each group there was far more variety—different classes, styles of rig and hull types. Eventually there were other more practical reasons for taking photographs of boats but all the time the idea of exploring the variety of subject matter within each category has stayed in my mind. Therefore this section of the book is intended to show the diversity from boat to boat as well as from rig to rig.

It should be noted that the term *rig* describes the manner in which a vessel's masts and sails are arranged. Many boats also get their identification by the style and construction of their hulls. A catboat, for example, is a hull type as well as a rig. If a boat has the rig of a catboat but not the characteristic hull, she can only be described as "cat rigged." There are variations of all kinds of boats. Producing the best of a type may be one goal, but making a variation—for better or worse—is more likely. And, adds to the variety.

ELEANOR is a Beetle cat, one of 3000 built since 1920.

Catboats

A classic catboat has three essential characteristics—shoal draft, a very broad beam, and a single mast set far up in the bow. Most catboats are gaff-rigged, have large outboard "barn door" rudders and are centerboarders, although some keel cats exist. There is a lovely roundness to the hull—some of the nicest curves in boatbuilding are found here, especially noticeable in coamings. The exact origin of the catboat is in doubt, but they appeared in the mid 1800s as workboats on Narrangansett Bay and the waters of Cape Cod and also New Jersey and New York. Many of the boats seen today date back to the 1910s and 20s and with a new interest in tradition they are also available in fiberglass, their character pretty much intact. Imagine, a fiberglass boat with mast hoops!

GYPSY is a Barnegat Bay type with a low, flat sheer and shrouds with spreaders. The curve in the bow is uncommon. Crosby cats *TANG* and *CATHY ANN*, opposite, are the more familiar New England style.

Sloops and Cutters

Most sailboats are sloops—single masted with a mainsail and jib—although a few such as the famous Friendship sloops may carry two headsails (jib and fore-staysail). The difference between a sloop and a cutter is often confusing. In the days when sloops with broad, shallow hulls were called "skimming dishes," the rival cutters were deep and extremely narrow and "cut" through the water. Later it was said that a cutter's mast was stepped farther aft than on a sloop, nearly amidships. A cutter is now thought of as a single masted boat with two or more headsails—a pointless distinction perhaps, but the term usually refers to older boats which may have some of the ealier characteristics as well, or to similar boats from Europe where cutters are more widely used. Sloop rigged boats come in a great assortment of hull styles and sail plans, often with a remarkably varied choice of sails for the area of the foretriangle.

HARDTACK, a 1939 design was un-typical of any style or period but proved to be a fast and able boat. The Islander 29 and Columbia 36 are more recent sloops in fiberglass.

A year after she was built, the cutter *HIGHLAND LIGHT* set a course record in the 1932 Bermuda Race of just under three days, which held for 24 years. She was given to the U.S. Naval Academy in 1939 and continued sailing until the late 1960s.

SILVER NIGHT is a splendid English cutter, narrow and deep.

Little is known about the gaff-rigged *LOTUS*. Possibly she was a Herreshoff design, at least the owners liked to think so. *FREYA* was a characteristic Norwegian double-ender. Both boats came to misfortune—*LOTUS* rotted away on a muddy river bank and *FREYA*, shortly after she was sold, caught fire and sank.

SANDBAGGERS

The shortened rig of the sandbagger SHADOW is only a suggestion of the enormous sail plans of these wide, shallow racers of the middle and late 1800s. To provide stability each boat carried many 50-pound bags of sand and a dozen husky crew members who, in addition to shifting their own weight at each tack, were obliged to take the sandbags with them. When the use of movable ballast was eventually prohibited, these extreme boats disappeared.

The magnificent sandbagger ANNIE, built in 1880, is preserved at Mystic Seaport. Her hull is 29 feet overall but it is nearly 70 feet from the tip of her bowsprit to the end of the boom. Her sail area is 1,313 square feet. SHADOW has a 22 foot hull with an 11 foot beam and once had a 20 foot bowsprit. She, and some others, had interchangeable cat and sloop rigs.

Take away that square box cabin and behold—an antique racer! The 27 foot *TIGER* and a sandbagger from Brooklyn named *BELLA* had a big race off Bridgeport, Conn. on June 22, 1870—a course of ten miles to a windward mark and back. The purse was $1500 per side with other betting estimated at over $50,000. *TIGER* was the pride of Bridgeport and many people turned out for a gala day to watch the race from a large excursion boat with a band playing. But they were disappointed. *TIGER* lost—by 39 seconds, although she had led by 31 seconds at the mark.

HOBGOBLIN

STARSAL

Present day sloops for racing and cruising include the Ensign class *REDHEAD*, upper left, the Shark class *MAAGEN II*, lower left, both of fiberglass, and *PALAWAN*, above, custom built of aluminum.

One of the largest fiberglass ocean racers thus far, the 61 foot *SORCERY* is a low displacement, tall rigged design from Canada. She has done well in racing, particularly when the wind was light and aft.

WINSOME, a Rhodes Reliant imported from Hong Kong.

All Yawls

The yawl is the second most popular rig, after the sloop. Although yawls and ketches are often defined together and occasionally confused, a yawl tends to be more like a sloop with a small mizzenmast added on. Conversions back and forth are not unusual. Olin Stephens' very successful *DORADE* and *STORMY WEATHER*, built in 1930 and 1934, started the trend toward yawls in ocean racing where Alden schooners had previously dominated. In the 1966 Bermuda Race more than half the fleet, 92 of 167, were yawls. However, changes in the rating rules since then have favored the sloop rig and yawls are now seen less often in racing events. Of course not all sailing is racing, and the two masted boat still has an advantage in that the sail area can be conveniently subdivided according to wind strength or increased with additional sails.

WELKIN, built in Argentina.

Lower right, *STORMY WEATHER*—winner of the Transatlantic and Fastnet Races in 1935.

When yawls became popular, many older boats were converted to the new rig. *BLUE SMOKE*, below, was originally a New York Forty, a class of one-design sloops built in 1916 for the New York Yacht Club. Forty was the waterline length—they were 59 feet overall and there were 13 of them.

One of the advantages of the yawl can be seen in this view of *ESCAPADE*. A large staysail can be set between the masts for reaching and running. In fact, the mizzenmast is often more useful for setting this sail than for the mizzen itself. Frequently yawls are seen with every possible sail set except the mizzen, which may make sense in sailing practice but leaves the boat looking incomplete. In this camera angle *ESCAPADE's* mizzenmast appears much taller than it really is.

A yawl that is gaff-rigged on both masts is now seldom seen. This one is named *W. C. FIELDS*. The combination of gaff-rigged main and Marconi mizzen was used for a time on some yawls and also ketches.

KLANG was built at Falmouth, England and has much English character. She's a lovely boat for cruising but the disadvantage of the gaff rig for racing is apparent here. Taller masts, Marconi-rigged, can reach winds higher up and allow for the setting of larger spinnakers and staysails.

GOOD NEWS raced successfully under several owners on both the East and West coasts. She was changed to a sloop in 1968 and later given to the Maine Maritime Academy at Castine.

Always a grand sight, the 71-foot *COTTON BLOSSOM IV* was one of the leading racers on Long Island Sound and offshore during the 50s and 60s. She was built in 1926 and converted from a cutter to a yawl in 1952. Now she's a charter boat in the Caribbean.

GERONIMO buries her rail in the sea off Block Island.

The yawls *PUFFIN* and *INVERNESS* are heading for Martha's Vineyard in an overnight race.

Two views of *TICONDEROGA*

The Ketch Rig

Ketches have had a steady following but without any periods of major popularity. They are aesthetically pleasing—the large mizzen gives a sturdy, balanced appearance which is often lacking in a yawl. Prior to and just after World War II they tended to be heavily built, husky looking boats for cruising although some were notable in racing such as *CHANTEYMAN* and the great *TICONDEROGA*. The later ketches *MERMAID* and *ROSA II* attracted attention and along with the 30 foot Seawind contributed to a new interest in the rig. The Seawind, designed by Thomas Gillmer, was the first ketch in fiberglass (1960)—one of them sailed around the world. Many builders offer fiberglass cruising ketches now and a few large custom designed ketches have been prominent ocean racers.

A variation known as the wishbone rig first appeared on a ketch named *VAMARIE* in 1933. It is visually intriguing and partisans claimed many advantages, but the rig was never widely accepted. *GOLDEN LION* and *STORMSVALA* are good examples. *SYRA*, above, started with this modernized version of the wishbone rig and later was converted to a yawl.

The clipper bow is one of the loveliest forms and sets the the style of *KARINA*, built in 1968, and *ROSA II*, opposite.

While many sailing yachts are designed to get favorable ratings, often at the expense of their looks, the naval architects M. Rosenblatt & Son chose to create a boat of their own "with aesthetic appeal as the primary goal." The success and reward of this objective is clear in *ROSA II*.

Left, *OSPREY* and *CHANTEY*—contrasting types.

Who could resist this delightful double-ender named *PENDRAGON?*

The ketch with dark sails wing and wing is *RON*, built in Scotland.

Motorsailers are meant to combine
some of the qualities of powerboat-
ing and sailing. The ketch rig is suitable for their more substantial hulls.
CRUSADER is built of steel.

EQUATION is one of the big ocean
racing ketches. The high aspect ratio
of her sails, typical of present designs, leaves a look of unused space
between the masts. The racing success of this 68 foot aluminum boat
is inspiring more ketch-rigged racers.

The ketch rig also appears on tri-
marans. *TROIKA* is appropriately
named.

Schooners

The schooners seen today are usually two masted boats. The second mast is the mainmast even if there are more than two. Three, four and five masted schooners were common in the late 1800s as cargo carriers. Some had six and the *THOMAS W. LAWSON*, built in 1902, was the only vessel to have seven masts. She was 385 feet overall and lasted just five years.

The two masted schooner was once the preferred rig for ocean racing. In 1930 the Bermuda Race had 30 of them in a fleet of 42 but their decline began soon after. Many continued in use as cruising boats and now schooner fanciers of a new generation are racing these remaining boats and other traditional types. A few new schooners are still being built.

The 78 foot *SEA GYPSY* is one of John Alden's fine schooners.

Opposite, *CHANTEY*, a classic Atkin design, and *CAROLINE*, by Lawley.

Staysail schooners *CHAUVE SOURIS* and *NIÑA*. One of the early staysail schooners, *NIÑA* won the transatlantic race to Spain the year she was built, 1928. She was successful in ocean racing events long after the time of schooners and in 1962 won the Newport to Bermuda Race.

A few schooners like *PHOEBE BENEDICT* had Marconi foresails.

TALARIA, called a Marco Polo, was designed in the 1940s as an ocean cruiser and is certainly unlike earlier three masters.

SUSAN ANN, right, has perhaps the most familiar schooner rig—a Marconi main and gaff foresail. There seems to be no name for this combination.

BLACKFISH, opposite, was one of my favorites. About sixteen hours after this picture was taken she lost her keel in a storm and capsized. All aboard reached shore in her dory.

The 104 foot *AMERICA* was launched on May 3, 1967 at East Boothbay, Maine. She re-creates the famous 1851 racing schooner whose victory over 17 English yachts led to the America's Cup Races. 70,000 board feet of lumber and 10,000 pounds of fastenings went into the new vessel. At first she had old style hatches, deadeyes, a colossal tiller and a six-bar capstan matching the original *AMERICA* for a documentary film. These later gave way to more modern arrangements.

73

TAMARACK from Gloucester, docking at Mystic Seaport.

Tradition and Character

The boats in this category include those with working origins, regional types, historic vessels, and variations of them. Traditional boats have usually been functional and some have changed very little. Sometimes when a working boat was altered to a yacht or a yacht patterned after a working boat, the result was less successful than the original. After all, different functions were introduced. However there have been many satisfying adaptations. "Character" is attributed to honest designs that have outlasted their period, but the term "character boat" is often condescending and may suggest a deliberate quaintness or inefficiency. This does describe some, but the success of traditional boats historically has been in their performance. These boats may come together now for events such as the Heritage Race at Block Island and the Mayor's Cup Race at New York City. With a diversity of types the contests are inevitably quite informal but they are fun and stimulate further interest in the boats.

The topsail schooner *SHENANDOAH*, launched in 1964, was built from the plans of the 1849 U.S. Revenue Cutter *JOE LANE*. She is operated as a charter vessel, making cruises off Cape Cod. She has no engine but is pushed through harbors by her motorized yawlboat.

ST. LAWRENCE II is a school ship for Canadian sea cadets and sails on Lake Ontario. Note the painted gunports! *BLACK PEARL*, opposite, is one of the well-known sights of Narragansett Bay. Both these boats are brigantines by the current definition—a two masted vessel square rigged on the foremast and schooner rigged on the mainmast. A true brigantine also had square topsails on the main-mast, but there never were many true brigantines.

BLACK PEARL is about half the length of the trading vessels of this type, which were first known as hermaphrodite brigs. She was designed as a private yacht for her builder, no doubt with her unique appearance as a prime reason for the rig.

LITTLE JENNIE is a true bugeye, built in 1884, and is one of the oldest yachts sailing. The bugeyes were originally workboats used in the Chesapeake Bay oyster industry and are now rare. They had canoe-shaped hulls, graceful clipper bows, and pointed sterns which later acquired square platforms above known as "patent sterns." Their triangular sails on sharply raked masts were in use long before the Marconi rig became a yachting standard. Raked masts have also appeared on other Cheaspeake types—schooners, skipjacks and log canoes.

PRIVATEER is often mistaken for a bugeye by yachtsmen but the Chesapeake Bay watermen call her type a "three-sail bateau." Her rig is the same but her hull, instead of having the round bilges of a bugeye, is V-bottomed like a skipjack. In this view the aftermast appears to be the taller one, but it isn't.

THUNDERBIRD, opposite, is a Norwegian double ended cutter of the Colin Archer type, designed for the weather of the North Sea. The added cabin house, while nicely built, does not suit her rugged style.

CLEARWATER, below, a full-size reproduction, is a composite of the Hudson River sloops of the 1800s—wide centerboard cargo boats and packets. Unlike other replicas used in chartering, she is sailed by a troupe of folk-singers who give concerts to dramatize campaigns against water pollution and is also used in other environmental projects.

The Friendship sloops, built in Friendship, Maine and other towns on Muscongus Bay, were used by New England lobster fishermen beginning in the late 1880s. The larger boats up to 40 feet or more carried a gaff topsail, although most were smaller and without a topmast. Yachtmen admired and acquired these boats but usually shortened the rigs a bit, thereby reducing their sailing qualities. Interest in Friendship sloops has continued to the present and there is an annual regatta for the original boats and replicas.

JOLLY BUCCANEER, above, a large Friendship at 45 feet, was built in 1909.

These two views show the latest schooner replica, the 125 foot *BILL OF RIGHTS* launched in June 1971. Her lines were suggested by the 1856 schooner *WANDERER* which was owned by a syndicate of New York Yacht Club members and later used as a contraband boat—the cargo included slaves who were ostensibly being liberated to the North but actually sold there as indentured servants. The new boat, built for chartering, gives the passengers a better time.

Man the main clew garnets, buntlines and leechlines
Tend the tacks and sheets
Set taut both lifts and belay
Clear away the tack jigger
Slack tacks and sheets, clew up
Belay

THE TRAINING SHIP
Eagle

The last reminders of the age of square rigged merchant ships are the training vessels maintained by several maritime nations. All but a few of these were built after that age. The U.S. Coast Guard's *EAGLE* was one of three training ships built for the German Navy in the 1930s and was taken as a reparation after World War II. *EAGLE* is a 295 foot bark—a complicated apparatus on which cadets learn to work individually as well as in a team. Their skills or shortcomings are more quickly evident in the handling of a ship like this than in many conventional ones. Training in a wind-powered vessel is economical and is an experience in our sea-going heritage. The military aspects seems less offensive than in other areas.

Hauling and hoisting is all done by hand power, as is the steering. There is no shortage of hands.

EAGLE carries 23 sails—10 squaresails, four headsails, six staysails, a spanker and a gaff topsail—a total of 21,350 square feet.

Training ships built since World War II include ten barkentines of about 130 feet built by Finland for the U.S.S.R., a large bark built by West Germany for herself and a barkentine for Indonesia, an East German brigantine, the 370 foot *ESMERALDA* built by Chile and the Argentine full-rigged ship *LIBERTAD*. England's Sail Training Association commissioned a pair of 3-masted topsail schooners in 1966 and '68. Some of the world's training vessels take part in the biennial Tall Ships Race.

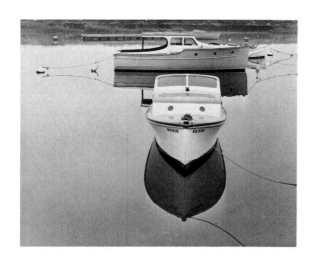

POWER

Unlike a sailboat, a power boat is not quite natural to the water. It brings to the water something of the land, but then so do people. And there are far more people who take to power boats than there are sailors. I have come to think of power boats in two basic categories—automotive and architectural.

Speedboats, runabouts and some of the small cruisers are really cars on the water and automotive influence has always been unmistakable in their engineering, production and styling. A primary consideration is speed, but while the world record for power boat speed is now over 285 mph, few stock speedboats do much more than 50, and they require immense horsepower to do even that. Nor are many of them able to maintain that speed in a chop. However, 25 to 40 mph in a small boat *feels* fast and in this case one doesn't compare it to a car—the sensation is perhaps closer to the same speed on a bicycle.

The architectural vessels are the cabin cruisers and yachts built with greater accommodations, their designs often following the concurrent styles of residential buildings. Enormous yachts of the past, elegantly finished and furnished, are thought of as "palatial" while present-day boats are advertised as having the comforts of home. Home and boat feature more glass to look through and "outdoor living" is provided by the patio and the flying bridge deck. Power cruisers have become summer cottages for many people, especially since some modern marinas offer so many recreational facilities that there is hardly a need to go away in the boat.

Usually, power boating is a means for doing something else—fishing, water skiing, visiting an anchorage filled with more boats or another marina, or some kind of racing such as a predicted log contest. The purpose of entertaining business clients, real or merely claimed, on tax-deductible yachts also keeps many owners in boating and many boat builders in business. And for a decidedly smaller number of persons a power boat is a platform for marine photography.

A medium size cruiser, *SCRIMSHAW* is a Chris-Craft Sea Skiff with an added flying bridge.

This is a typical cruiser of the 1950s, name unknown. The great butterfly of bow wave and spray shows why a displacement hull uses a large amount of power just to break the resistance of the water.

Inland boating—a runabout on Lake Dardanelle in Arkansas.

This brightly varnished inboard launch is tastefully functional and has the appeal of a boat that the owner worked on himself, something often lacking in larger, impersonal yachts.

The 50 foot Hatteras convertible fisherman *EXCITE* is an impressive example of current styling and big boat fiberglass construction.

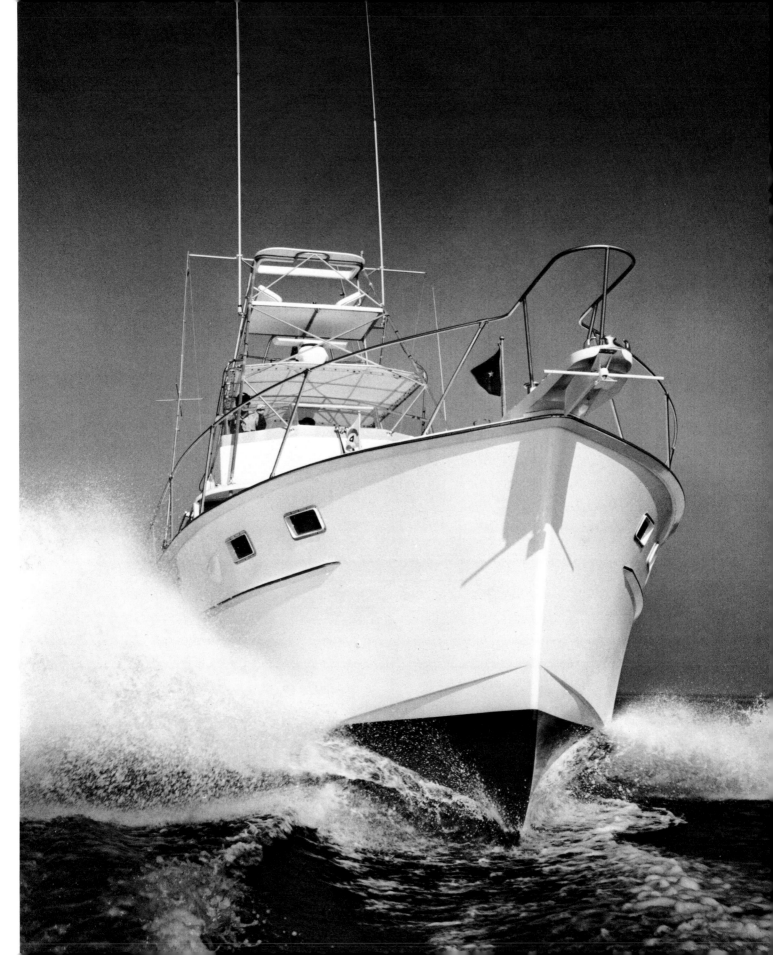

TWO LOVELY ANTIQUES. The lake steamer is *SCUDDER*, 38 feet and built in 1903 at Kingston, Ontario. *SUWANEE* is a 1908 speed launch at the Thousand Islands. 32 feet long and 4 feet wide, she does 30 mph with a 40 hp engine. Riding in this boat and slicing into waves is a unique sensation, quite unlike boating today. A lot can be said for narrow hulls.

In the summer of 1958 two boats designed by C. Raymond Hunt were involved in the America's Cup Trials. One was the 12 meter sloop *EASTERNER* and the other was her 23 foot tender. Of the two, the tender had the greater success. This boat, which could do 40 knots through rough water, had a deep V shape in her hull extending to the stern with lengthwise strakes on each side. She was the inspiration for the Bertram boats and the other Deep V designs developed for offshore powerboat racing. The Zekeboat, above, is the one of this type adapted for the non-racing public. (A picture of the original Hunter 23 is on page 172.)

FISHING

Fishing is the pastime of a large percentage of boat owners and great numbers of non-boat owners as well. No matter where people fish—off a bridge or offshore, from a rowboat or a yacht—there is a universal contentment just in being there.

SPORTFISHING BOATS. Two views of *DADSON*. The outriggers and tuna towers of these boats are for me a pleasing, visual equivalent to rigging on a large sailboat. But if a sport is a contest between willing opponents, sportfishing is no more a sport than hunting.

WORKING BOATS

People who argue unprovable questions might debate whether the first boat was for work or pleasure. Early man probably found enjoyment in that first raft of logs but he may have built it for the task of transporting himself across a river. The performance of needed services has been the primary function of boats throughout history. Until the end of their reliance on wind power, American working vessels strongly influenced the yachts of their day —the 1851 racing schooner *AMERICA*, for an example, was a sister ship of the New York pilot boats. Sailing yachts and commercial vessels have long since gone their separate ways but I like the way of each.

I like the honesty of working boats. Most often they are practical designs, each intended for a particular assignment. Styling may change over the years, but not just for the sake of style, and fads are less evident than in pleasure boats. Embellishments take the form of wholly separate ornaments such as the gold eagle on each tugboat of the Dalzell Line. Other kinds of decoration are done with paint—an elaborate technique called "graining" on some tugs gives a stunning effect of brightwork over a steel pilot house.

Counter stern and rudder of the freighter *EXCHEQUER* and *JAMES HAMEL*, a tanker.

DALZELL 2. One tug can move two barges loaded with 40 railway cars.

Tugs *ESSO NEW JERSEY* and *MARIE J. TURECAMO* guiding the tanker *BERG-LJOT* through New York's East River. The Brooklyn Bridge and skyline of Manhattan are in the background.

Fishing boats and falling snow. Seasonal changes are familiar to most working vessels. These scenes are in Saugatuck and East Norwalk, Connecticut.

Passenger-carrying hydrofoil vessels have had considerably more success in Europe. This small Dutch built *COMMUTABOAT* powered by outboard motors was demonstrated in the United States in 1962 for commuting over metropolitan area waters.

The oyster dredging skipjacks of the Chesapeake are the last American fleet of sailing workboats. They are very distinctive vessels ranging in length from 39 to 60 feet with beams of 13 to 20 feet. But the Maryland conservation law requiring that oysters be dredged under sail has had several changes and now the working skipjacks which once numbered 1500 are down to less than 40. None has been built since 1956. These three are *SEA GULL, ROSIE PARKS* and *GENEVA MAY*.

RACING

When two or more boats compete, sailing becomes a sport. While most people prefer their sailing to be a relaxation free from rivalry and tension, there's an undeniable thrill in overtaking another boat, especially if the other skipper is doing his best to prevent it. Racing sailors are usually competitive in other fields and bring this sense to their sailing.

For pictures, action is more likely in racing. Competitive skippers drive their boats harder and have full crews to keep all sails properly trimmed. But racing may also be the occasion for a total absence of action—an entire fleet may be becalmed for hours with sails wilting in humid sunlight. And who but a racing crew would spend an afternoon in a dull, saturating drizzle? Remarkable sailing skills may come into play when the wind is faint or flukey, but they are less apt to translate into pictures.

I follow boat races enthusiastically although the tactics and performances are really incidental to me. Instead, I see a race as a chance to photograph an individual boat in a special situation or to see two or three boats in some relation to one another, perhaps repeating a pattern or with contrasting shapes and diagonals. Interesting opportunities come right after the start of a race when boats are still in close quarters and there is a fast interchange of positions in tacking or overtaking sequences. Spinnakers and other light sails are used most often in racing—some people may tire of spinnaker pictures but I haven't. While I can assume that racing sailors are less absorbed with shapes and patterns, they may frequently find some informative value in these pictures, even if it isn't my primary aim. People look at pictures to find the things that interest them.

SNIPE

The Snipe first appeared in 1931 and for many years was the most popular racing class—nearly 20,000 have been built. But this number has now been far exceeded by such smaller classes as the Sailfish, Sunfish and Snark.

ATLANTIC

The Atlantic is a handsome boat. 99 of them were built in Germany from 1928 to 1930 and they raced mainly on Long Island Sound for 25 years. In 1955 when the wooden boats were aging and difficult to maintain, the class association approved the conversion to fiberglass hulls. But 30 feet is long for a day racer and the fleet remains fairly small.

They sure did!

LIGHTNING

The Lightning was first built in 1938 and became extremely popular not only for racing but for day sailing as well. The hull is somewhat boxy but the boat is photogenic, especially with the spinnaker which is nicely round and relatively large.

STAR

One of the oldest classes, the Star was designed in 1911 and originally had a sliding gunter rig (gaff almost parallel to the mast). Later there was a short Macroni rig which was then changed to the present, taller rig. No spinnaker is used. Not a family boat, the Star is low, wet and fast.

INTERNATIONAL TEMPEST

The trend has been toward more action and performance in racing classes. The International Tempest, an English design, is spectacularly fast—a planing boat that requires considerable agility in the crew. The boat was introduced in 1963 and selected for the 1972 Olympics.

THISTLE

Planing adds another dimension to sailing. The Thistle, designed in 1945, was the first one-design planing boat to become successful in the U.S. and is basically a blown up version of the International-14. A Thistle has no decking. It's a good family boat but also exciting. A good wind is required for it to photograph well.

Off Soundings

Twice a year, in the Spring and Fall, the Off Soundings Club sponsors a weekend of racing—starting at New London, Conn. and sailing either to Gardiner's Bay or Block Island. It's one of the largest events in the East with over 200 boats.

The Off Soundings fleet is varied. Among the modern racer-cruisers one may see older boats and some less familiar rigs. The series is noted not only for the sailing but for conviviality after the race. The Off Soundings Club was formed in 1933 "to promote good fellowship between men actively interested in sailing." A member who buys a motorboat instead of sailing is automatically dropped.

The spinnaker trio is *SOUFFLÉ*, *MERIDIAN* and *CHRISADA*. Rounding the mark are *WINDLASSIE*, *EMILY*, *GINN-MILL* and (close-up view) *SEA DREAMER*.

Bermuda Race

The major ocean racing event in the East is the Newport to Bermuda Race, held every two years. It began in 1906 with three entries and is now so popular that the fleet must be limited to a manageable size. 178 boats sailed in the 1972 race.

A typical race start—Class C in 1970 with *WANDELAAR* and *H.M.S. DAY* in the foreground. *CARINA*, opposite, was the winner that year. The 1972 sloop *LA FORZA DEL DESTINO* is in her first ocean race, headed for Bermuda.

The German yawl *HAMBURG VII* is one of the international entries in the Bermuda Race. Participants may encounter all kinds of conditions from great calms to 60 knot squalls on a passage that averages four to five days. *FIGARO III*, opposite, has been in many ocean races but this view was taken on Long Island Sound during snow flurries.

Block Island Week

Block Island is the scene of a newer event held by the Storm Trysail Club and patterned after England's Cowes Week. The island's immense harbor can accommodate many boats, and nearly 200 come in feeder races from different sailing areas for a week of competition. Block Island also provides a suitable racing course—around the island. The unknown factor is the fog which comes frequently and is either a challenge or a problem. Being at a small island in the fog is sensuous. But it *is* a lot of fog.

The boats in these views include *CIMBRIA, ILLUSION, PUFF, THUNDERHEAD* and *WILD GOOSE.*

Heritage Race

At Newport, Rhode Island in 1964, several schooner owners who had sailed there to watch the Cup Races held an unofficial race of their own—for schooners. Their enjoyment led to plans for a larger event which became the American Heritage Race at Block Island. Though often spoiled by poor weather, the event has inspired other competitions for traditional boats.

MADRIGAL followed by *SILVER HEELS*, opposite, and leading *ADVENTURER*, above. Right, *TAMARACK* and Friendship sloop *TANNIS II*.

GRETEL II. Interior of a cup challenger—a view from the mast to the bow.

America's Cup Racing

Sailboat racing is not a spectator sport—it gives its immediate satisfaction only to those who are actual participants. Even so, thousands of people involve themselves every three or four years in the America's Cup Races, an extraordinary series which is ultimately sailed by only two skippers and about twenty crewmen. Before that happens, new boats are designed, built and equipped at great cost, trial races are held to select a defender of the Cup and foreign boats compete for the right to challenge. Because the competing 12-meter sloops, 60 to 70 feet overall, are built to a formula that allows some latitude in their construction, the races are not only contests for sailors but also for designers and sailmakers. Unfortunately, after the excitement of the trial races and the publicity and speculation they generate, the final races have tended to be anti-climactic—Americans have consistently had the right combination to win with ease and in the few cases where it was thought that the American boat was not really the fastest, superior crew work was decisive. More and more observers have come to root for the challengers if only in the hope of seeing closer matches. When possession of the Cup is really in doubt, there is certain to be remarkable racing.

WEATHERLY was one of the best looking 12-meter contenders. Beauty is hardly essential in the 12-meter formula and little effort is made for color or distinctive embellishments. An exception was the unsuccessful sloop *FRANCE* in 1970 which had a set of spinnakers emblazoned with the coats of arms of French provinces. But the most distressing development from a pictorial standpoint was very sound for racing—putting the winches and crew below deck to get their weight down low. No longer do we see any human activity except during sail changes—the boats simply sail along looking empty with only the helmsmen and perhaps navigators in view. The crew working on the deck of *CONSTELLATION*, like a frieze on a Grecian vase, is a thing of the past.

CONSTELLATION follows *INTREPID* closely around a whistle buoy.

DAME PATTIE and *COLUMBIA*. On a calm, hot day during the Cup Trials of 1967 when *INTREPID* and *CONSTELLATION* were drawing the spectator fleet, *COLUMBIA*, the California boat, went off by herself and eventually met the Australian challenger *DAME PATTIE*. The two sailed together briefly with each crew trying to look nonchalant while making careful observations of the other. When the distant spectators saw what was happening they came charging out en masse, whereupon the two twelves quickly parted: New York Yacht Club rules forbid early contact with the challenging boat. *COLUMBIA* later lost the chance to defend the cup to *INTREPID* which easily defeated the Australians in the final series.

The scene of cup race activity is Newport, Rhode Island—historic seaport and summer home of extravagant wealth. Opulence is out of fashion now and the simpler colonial architecture of Newport is being restored. Replica of *H.M.S. ROSE* looms from the waterfront in a view from Pelham St.

VALIANT, built for the 1970 competition, was expected to be the defender but had only a few victories over *INTREPID* in the trials, one of them seen here. Although her sail number is 24, she is actually the 23rd American 12-meter—superstition had precluded a number thirteen.

HERITAGE had a varnished hull that made her the most attractive twelve meter boat of 1970. She and her crew were very popular in Newport but given little hope to win.

Watching an America's Cup race presents many difficulties of distance and perspective. Nevertheless thousands of onlookers strain for a glimpse of the racers through some of the most congested boating they ever encounter. Mostly, it's a social occasion.

In the 1970 Cup races, *INTREPID* (larger silhouette) trailed the Australian *GRETEL II* more than once, giving future challengers their best encouragement to keep trying.

INTREPID and foredeck crew in 1967.

PLACES

Boating is a means to get away—to lose the land in favor of clear open water or to re-visit at selected and somewhat detached locations. The problem is that people who are making the land more of a thing to get away from are doing the same to the water. In the range of metropolitan areas the shore is overdeveloped, waterways are less appealing, anchorages are crowded and commercial marinas exist primarily for consumers of gas. Increasingly, owners keep their boats in more distant places and commute to them by faster transportation. In time the places to "get away from it all" are filled with people who bring it all with them.

But the memorable place is not necessarily far away nor is it always an entire area. It is usually remembered in a few impressions—fragmentary views that are symbols or comments on the location or perhaps not at all typical. They may also be observations with little geographic reference. If I come back from Gloucester with a picture of a sea gull, it's also a picture of a place as long as I remember the view. The nearest harbor is another place.

Block Island is a place all its own. The familiar view shows New Harbor with boats rafted together and characteristic houses in the distance. The fishing boat hulk and old windmill at Champlin's Dock are more remote suggestions of the island's atmosphere.

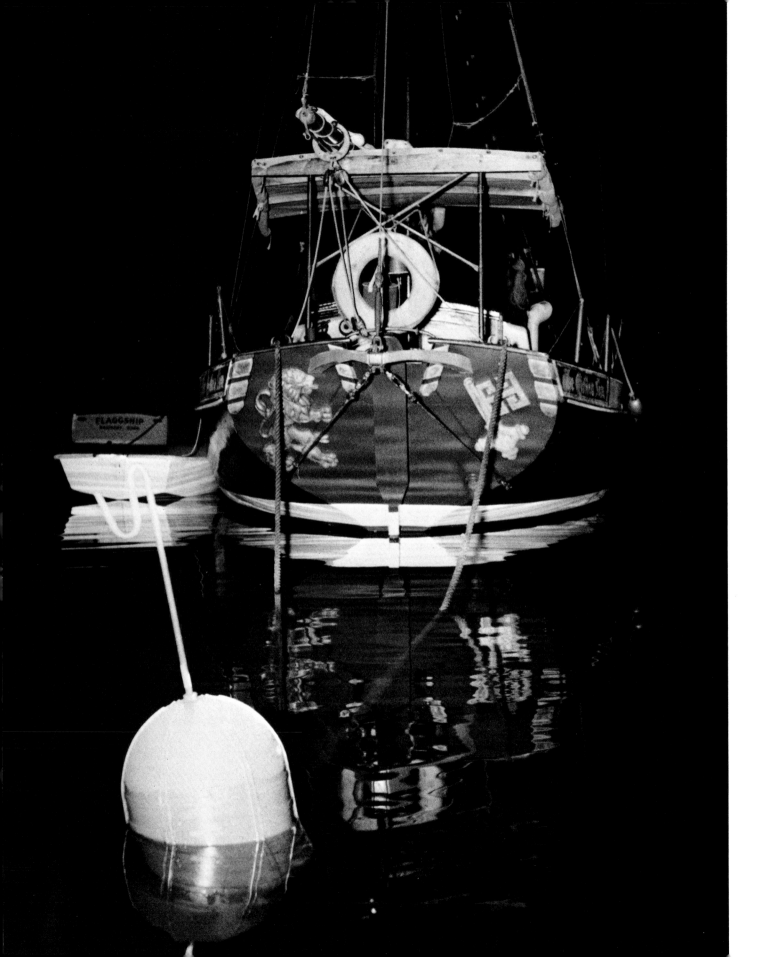

This view might be anywhere—especially anywhere in the Chesapeake with all its creeks and inlets. It's the Chester River just east of Crumpton, Maryland.

Nighttime in the harbor and the *GOLDEN LION* sleeps.

The crew of *AFTA* is performing the final skill for a Sunday sail. The other sailors are Dorrie Barlow and Jo Ray, owner of *HARDTACK* (page 38).

You can walk ashore
when the tide goes out.

Or maybe clam.

The larger-than-life figure is mounted over the door of an East Gloucester antique shop called The Bluejacket.

Visitors to Wiscasset, Maine will remember the great schooner hulks of the *HESPER* and *LUTHER LITTLE*. These four-masters, both over 200 feet, were built in 1917 and 18 and used profitably in the coal and lumber trades. They were still in good condition by 1932, but there was no longer a demand and they were sold at auction. *HESPER* was bought for only $600. The two vessels were towed to Wiscasset where they have remained.

Two kinds of fishing craft pass in the narrow breachway which separates Galilee from neighboring Jerusalem. The working boats are usually named after wives or children—*PRISCILLA*, *LUCY M.* or *JERRY & JIMMY*. The sport boat names are often dreams of glory like *ABDUCTOR* and *INVADER*. The sea gulls here have as easy a life as a bird could want.

GALILEE

The fishing village of Galilee, Rhode Island, close to Point Judith, has some fifty commercial vessels that work the year around and a processing plant for fish meal and other by-products. In the summer Galilee is also a sport fishing center. Two annual tuna tournaments are held in September.

A cottage for sale.

THE RELICS OF STATEN ISLAND

For years the forgotten part of New York City was the borough of Richmond, better known as Staten Island, where there are still meadows and occasionally a small farm. Typical of neglect however is the wreckage of ships along parts of the shore—old tugboats, barges and others, broken and rotting, some burned above the high tide level and slimy below when the tide goes out. This is a graveyard of ships. The Statue of Liberty is nearby, facing the other way, and one is reminded of that inscription about "wretched refuse" and "Give me your tired . . . your huddled masses. . . ." But individually, these relics take on some historical fascination and maybe a grotesque kind of beauty. Or do you just get an eyesore?

An old Staten Island steam ferry, the *DONGAN HILLS* has a deck of wooden blocks. *GERTRUDE E. DAILEY* was a Hudson River and Erie Canal barge used for carrying grain. The Jonah-in-the-whale view shows a World War II leftover—a PT boat or air sea rescue craft.

Salvage yard along the Arthur Kill.

A ship's lifeboat in the grass.

The cross-section of a derelict tug shows construction techniques that might have been seen 75 years earlier when she was being built—heavy ceiling (inner planking) and oak ribs. Notice the treenails (wooden pin fastenings) in the lower section.

A FISH LOOKS
MOST LIKE A FISH
AT EITHER END

This section is a more personal view. It is more about pictures than boats even though all the views are related to boats or the shore. And it's mostly about photographic observation—about seeing, and noticing.

Photography is most effective as a medium for observing reality—for recording everyday sights or those seldom seen. Experience with a camera helps one to watch for things that happen quickly and to consider things that were there all along. Few of us really see much of what we look at, which is sad because noticing things with some thought takes a fairly small effort.

Abstract patterns are emphasized in these photographs showing the clipper bow of the famous ketch *TICONDEROGA* and a view from the crosstrees of the 295 foot bark *EAGLE*.

You see a sea serpent? Some ancient calligraphy? A modern stained glass window? I see a branch in the water—but an interesting branch.

To a sailor a properly secured line looks good because it's properly secured. But it also looks good because it's a good design—and that's a comment on function and appearance. Which is better looking, a square knot or a granny knot?

Not a fleeting moment, but you may never see it again. This picture of *PINA-FORE* could probably be faked in the darkroom. What makes it genuine, like an oriental rug, is the built-in but imperceptible flaw—in this case the ripples in the reflected bobstay and sheer.

The more usual, and distant, view of this object makes it seem light and delicate. Up close it is a heavy, massive structure which in fact weights 13 tons. It's a bell and light buoy, the same one as on Page 33.

These two photographs have in common the effect of distance created by secondary
elements. The fog picture would certainly be less effective without the man rowing.
And the ruins of a Newport summer house might look empty and two-dimensional
if that slightly magic window didn't show in the doorway.

Gentle waves of the Atlantic off the eastern coast of Long Island, taken from a Coast Guard helicopter.

The 40 foot cutter *FINN MacCUMHAILL* behind a large wave makes a view reminiscent of some old Japanese prints. Actually the wave was about three feet high and much nearer the camera. The picture was intentional once the wave was spotted although there was no certainty about the shape it would take. Unusual effects are often quite accidental, especially in action shots, but an element of luck can be anticipated or planned.

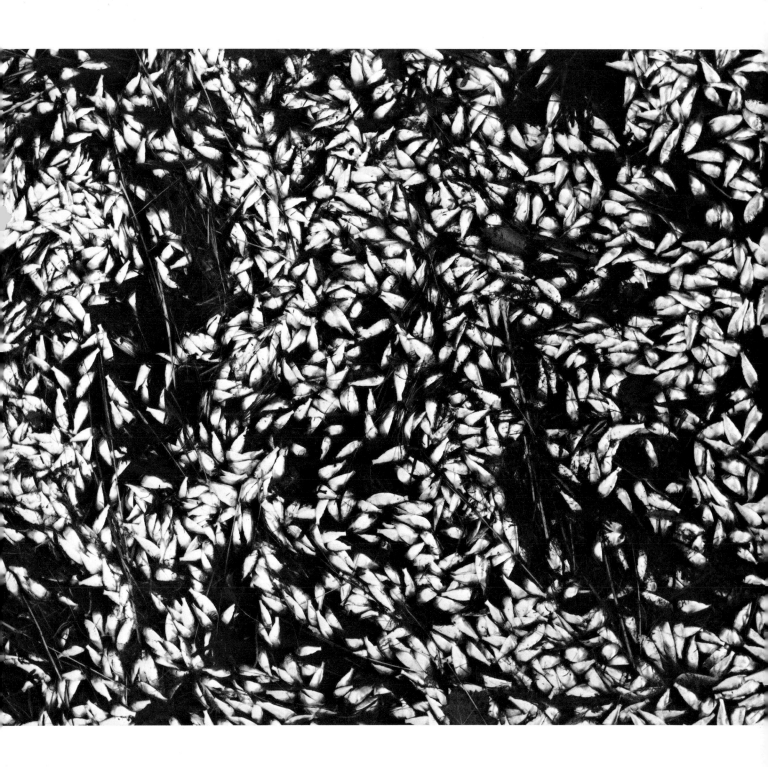

A fish looks most like a fish at either end.

Pictures on the Water

Camera operation and boat handling seem to draw on similar aptitudes. Quite a few boating people are interested in taking photographs on the water and many have asked me questions about equipment and techniques. This section is concerned with methods of marine photography along with opinions and a few experiences.

The elements that make good boating photographs are not really different from many other types of photography—the use of lighting, waiting for the right moment, being there at the right time, seeing the subject with some thought, planning ahead if necessary or making the most of some good luck. Some of these will be apparent in descriptions of the different kinds of pictures that follow.

SILVER NIGHT

This is essentially a portrait of a boat—the intent was to show this English cutter at her best. The wind was about 18 knots from the south in late afternoon. The combination of a wind direction and light direction was just right to produce a rounded shading on the sails. A normal lens was used at close range to preserve the graceful lines of the boat. I use a normal lens wherever possible unless there is a reason for a longer lens. Camera: Rolleicord.

THISTLE

A telephoto lens, like binoculars, reduces the distance between you and a boat you're looking at. In an off-the-bow view of that boat it also reduces the distance from the bow to the stern while leaving the beam unchanged. This is highly unflattering to the boat, giving it a tubby shape. But often the action of people aboard is enhanced by this "squeezed up" perspective and will offset the disadvantage to the boat. In this view of a Thistle planing at nearly 15 knots, the people hiking out make the picture. A Nikon camera with a 200 mm lens was used. It was a very gusty day with small craft warnings and the Thistle regatta had been cancelled—these sailors came out partly to have their picture taken. I cut across their bow, which is generally not done during a race. They were almost too close for a 200 mm lens—the photo shows the entire negative area.

In this photo of a fleet of Atlantic sloops coming home after a race it is unusual that none of the boats overlaps another (with one minor exception). This is the sort of thing that can't be planned. It isn't essential that boats not overlap, but in this shot the open sky area around each boat tends to emphasize the depth or distance in the picture. The normal lens also adds to this with its receding perspective.

SPECTATOR BOATS

Special purpose for a telephoto lens—creating an added feeling of congestion in a crowded spectator fleet. (Nikon, with 200 mm lens.) When you look at a group of boats from far away you are not aware of much distance between the nearest one and those further away. The telephoto lens transposes this lack of depth to close range. The eye sees this picture as a crowded scene and tends to overlook the squatty appearance of the boats which would be objectionable in separate views of each one. If you took the photo from a point very near the leading boat with a normal lens the other boats would diminish in size, as in the Atlantic photo.

SNIPE

The Snipe Class sloop was photographed with a Rolleicord—normal lens. The sailors were cooperating for the picture but I had to fend off their sail as they went by. This obviously is more a picture of the enjoyment of sailing than specifically of a Snipe. There is also a slight feeling of telephoto perspective because even though the picture was taken at close range it does not represent the total negative area. Thus, if a very small portion of a photo made with a normal lens is enlarged, taking it from the context of distance, the effect of a telephoto lens will be seen.

PINAFORE

About the only problem in photographing reflections is that you may not have a camera when you see them. The view of the sloop *PINAFORE* was taken from shore at the water's edge with a normal lens and the camera was held at water level to make the two images as nearly identical as possible. In the original square negative the mast and horizon intersect at the center, allowing considerable latitude in printing. Composing with a larger area of water naturally emphasizes the reflection.

CHESTER RIVER

The idyllic scene on the Chester River was spotted in the rear-view mirror of my car as I drove along a country road on the way home from Maryland. It was late in the afternoon and cloudy. A Nikon with a 200 mm lens was used—the compressed perspective is hardly noticeable, especially since the boat is in a nearly broadside view. When travel time permits, back roads and shore routes are far more rewarding photographically than superhighways.

GOLDEN LION

The night view of the *GOLDEN LION* at her mooring was taken from a dinghy with a Rolleicord and a flashbulb was used for illumination. Flash equipment mounted on cameras produces an angle of lighting that is usually undesirable and often unpredictable with shiny surfaces. But the results may sometimes be acceptable. The buoy and lighthouse lens on Page 29 were also taken with flash.

DAME PATTIE and COLUMBIA

Being where the picture is. This was not just a pretty type of photo but also had considerable news value, showing the first encounter of an American twelve meter (*COLUMBIA*) with the Australian cup challenger *DAME PATTIE* in the summer of 1967. The photo was taken at close range with a normal lens (Rolleicord). There were only the faintest puffs of wind but enough to fill the sails and carry the boats through glassy water, even with bow waves. The view demonstrates that it is possible to take a pleasing sailing photo in a poor breeze provided some element of interest is present. California sailors saw in this picture their hopes for a West Coast boat to defend the America's Cup and they ordered many prints.

WIDE ANGLE LENSES

A few pictures in this book were taken with a wide lens (28 mm with a Nikon). Wide angle lenses may be used for special effects but are mainly used when it is impossible to get back far enough for the desired view. The most logical occasions are when photographing boat interiors (*GRETEL II's* bow, page 128) and other views on board (*EAGLE*, page 86). Generally, I avoid wide angle lenses if possible—the distortion is too much (even though the human eye may see it that way too).

The picture of the salvage yard on Staten Island (page 00) was also taken with a wide angle lens. This was a view that I wanted to find but the problem was that my companion and I were barred from entering the yard by the watchman and a padlocked gate. Instead, we drove a short way down the highway and found a dirt road which looked like it might lead into the back of the yard. It did, but just before the yard there was a secluded spot where we suddenly came upon two New York City policemen in their squad car—relaxing with quart bottles of beer. This was as unexpected for us as the appearance of two photographers loaded with cameras must have been for them, but after a short conversation it was established that neither party was a threat to the other. And with that we entered the salvage yard and got the pictures.

PHOTOGRAPHING FROM A DINGHY

On several occasions I have seen the crew of a sailboat put someone with a camera into a dinghy, set him adrift, and then sail back and forth while he takes pictures of the boat. It is hard to do very much of anything in a dinghy and picture taking may be especially frustrating—there is little ability to maneuver and the boat being photographed may come too close or stay too far away. Any time a photographer is unable to control his position in relation to the subject, he at some disadvantage. Even so, this view from the dinghy is often the person's first full sight under sail of the boat he sails on. Sometimes if I have nothing else to do, I offer to tow his dinghy and invite him aboard my boat for a better view of his.

AERIAL PHOTOGRAPHY

There are a few pictures in this book taken from small planes and helicopters. This is not a frequent method for me and I have no special technique for it, except that here too I like to get close to the subject—a near normal lens makes a better perspective than a telephoto. Therefore, the pilot and I go as low as possible. It is extremely important that the pilot and photographer learn to work together as a team, and it is no surprise to me that a newspaper like the New York *Daily News* gives a credit line to the pilot as well as the photographer on their aerial photos. (For the record, the pilot who assisted in the aerial views in this book is Harvey Redak.)

Photographing from a helicopter has advantages. With care it can be done at certain angles fairly close to a boat under sail. However, sailors are justified in finding it objectionable.

The aerial views of tugboats (pages 102–103) and the yacht (page 90) were taken from the Manhattan Bridge in New York, a lovely vantage although at the time there were rules against taking photos on the bridge. Working photographers are inclined to disregard such regulations—the gentler among us will only consider if doing so will hurt anyone.

CLOUDS

I am not a great fancier of clouds in pictures. There are many formations that I like, and quite a few pictures are effective with clouds but they are not always necessary. I do not feel that a picture with clear, uninterrupted, deep blue sky will automatically be improved by a few clouds—in fact, I *like* clear, deep blue sky. I also like totally blank white sky. Both of these enable the eye to concentrate on the form of the immediate subject. Clouds may tend to complicate a picture, particularly if the subject itself is complicated. They are best with a foreground of simple, massive shapes. Another problem is that while those lovely big clouds that form with northwest wind make fine backgrounds when the sun is shining, the picture changes drastically when they cover the sun. There is no kind of light more useless to me for photographing a boat under sail than a sunny day with the sun behind a cloud—a completely overcast day is better than that. But sometimes an effect is worth waiting for —I followed *SEA GYPSY* (page 67) for about eight miles before the sun came out of a dramatic cover to light up this great schooner. Clouds may also require more composing of the picture if they are to appear in the right places. The view of *MAAGEN II* (page 48) shows an effective pattern—there is a curve of clouds that almost suggests wind filling the sails with light clouds against darker areas of sail and light sail against sky. The cloud on top of the mast is a finishing touch. Was it all planned? Probably not—except for a general awareness of the clouds. I was more likely watching the spinnaker and level of the bow.

One of the darkroom techniques that used to be popular and fortunately isn't done as much anymore is dubbing clouds into pictures that don't have any. Invariably, boat pictures of this sort look unconvincing. Having never accepted the need, I never learned the technique.

CAMERAS

Just about any type of camera can be used on the water but some are easier to use than others. They are the ones that are easier to use anywhere.

As noted before, most of the pictures in this book were taken with Rolleicords and Nikons. I no longer use Rolleicords. The 1955 model was excellent and I bought many of them second hand, but later models had a series of "improvements" that were unsuitable. The choice of 35mm came gradually with the need for telephoto lenses. While Nikon cameras and their companion Nikkormats are marvelous to work with, the proportions of 35mm are poor for many boat photographs. A heeling boat just doesn't fit very well into a tall narrow negative. I have tried several cameras that use telephoto lenses with larger film but never liked them. However, I am presently working with a new one that shows promise.

LENSES

Since sharpness is a requirement in a boat picture, the quality of a lens is important. One may put up with occasional camera disorders but a poor lens is chronic.

A handy lens, not previously mentioned, is a modest telephoto of about 85 to 105mm for a 35mm camera. It is enough to bring the subject (or the background) closer while keeping a pleasant perspective. Such a lens would be ideal for the boatman who doesn't want to get very close to other boats or who doesn't want to change lenses frequently.

FILM

Most of the pictures in this book were made on Kodak Panatomic-X film. Some of the earlier ones were taken with Kodak Verichrome Pan and the old Plus-X (not to be confused with the present film of that name). Tri-X was used for the Staten Island series.

FILTERS

A yellow filter used with black and white film will darken blue sky giving a contrast for clouds and sailboats. This filter is virtually required for marine pictures—without it the sky tends to be washed out. With control in the darkroom the contrast can be increased if desired, so there is really no need for orange or red filters.

The yellow filter serves an equally important role of protecting the lens from salt spray and can be used on cloudy days as well. Salt water can be rubbed off the less vulnerable filter with a handkerchief (for best results, lick the salt off first as you would with sunglasses).

PHOTOGRAPHING SAILBOATS IN A RACE

Groups of sailboats are generally photographed from points outside of a racing course. Many good views are seen near turning marks where one has a chance for head-on pictures without being in the way. A telephoto lens can be used to advantage—the squeezed-up perspective of converging boats often will make the action look more exciting and the competition closer. This is slightly fraudulent of course, but a normal lens may have a tendency to diminish the action, especially in showing sea conditions.

For pictures of individual racing boats or close-up views, the problem is to avoid interference with the boat being photographed and others coming up from astern which will be hindered by the photoboat's wake. A knowledgeably operated photoboat, familiar to the racers and small, can usually work inside the course. Confident sailors seldom object but there are occasional nervous types who gesture and babble at the sight of any motorboat. Caution and courtesy are obligations of anyone who comes close enough to boats to photograph them. Motorboats certainly can be offensive at times—more than once I have seen a succession of power cruisers in a predicted log contest plowing through a fleet of racing sailboats. But wind sailors have sometimes had an attitude of exclusive domain over the sailing water. That was doomed some time ago.

Crew members on racing boats are frequently in a position to take unique photographs. Unfortunately the best situations come into view when their services are needed in handling the boat.

Race Committee boats sometimes offer a spectacular view of action at the starting line, but that's about all. Being on a committee boat is a great gamble.

Press boats, when events warrant them, can be good or bad. Anyone who has been on a number of these comes to appreciate the few skippers who really know how to follow a race for the benefit of photographers.

MY BOAT

The boat I am currently using for marine photography is an Aquasport, a 22 foot fiberglass boat, entirely open, whose helm is a little aft of amidships. It has an unobstructed 360° view for taking pictures and can be operated simultaneously. It also has its limitations. There is no all-around boat for this work any more than there is an all-purpose camera. There are times when a much smaller boat would be better—for photographing in the midst of a fleet of small sailboats, for example. Other times a large boat with a flying bridge or even a tuna tower is desirable. I get on all kinds of boats but the Aquasport is a simple and practical one to own.

My previous motorboat, from which many of the photos in the book were taken, was a 17 foot wooden, inboard speedboat with a small shelter cabin. It had a lot of character and I did some elaborate painting and woodwork on it, but my needs outgrew it.

HEAD-ON VIEWS OF POWER BOATS

A head-on or nearly head-on picture of a power boat traveling at a good speed takes some planning in advance since the desired perspective requires shooting at close range. One method is to have the photoboat running directly ahead of the subject, slowing down a bit to reduce the wake at the moment a picture is taken, then speeding up quickly. The photoboat's wake spoils many pictures, detracting from the composition and revealing to the viewer how it was taken. In the view of *EXCITE* (page 93) there is some wake from the photoboat and it would be better without it. But a wake may sometimes be used to advantage for a "jumping" shot of one of the performance-type speedboats. Another method for head-on views is to cross in front of the oncoming power boat on nearly a right angle course. This will eliminate the photoboat's wake from the picture but it requires more precise timing and several passes to get a choice of shots. While it is possible for me to use both these techniques singlehandedly, this is one time when a helmsman on the photoboat is very handy. However, the whole procedure can be unnerving and there is no technique I would really recommend. A telephoto can be used at a distance if there is no concern about the lines of the boat.

COASTER　　　　　　　　　　*TAPPAN ZEE*

Hunter 23

Some years back, with my first motorboat, I had another technique for taking near head-on pictures of power boats. This involved stopping my boat in the water and arranging for the skipper of the subject boat to come barrelling down on a course at right angles to the way my boat was lying and pass the stern of my boat "as close as you can come"—by which I meant a few feet. I would lean over the stern and take one low angle view when the subject was still about 25 feet away and in the next few seconds, as it went by, shield the camera from the spray of the bow wave and brace myself for a free ride over the oncoming wake. They were big wakes too!—the boats were usually 40 to 50 footers and sometimes much larger. I learned this method gradually since few captains were willing to come as close as I wanted the first time and needed some assurance that my 17 foot boat wouldn't be swamped or flipped. Only once did my boat get hit. When photographing the Hunter 23, prototype of the Bertrams, the helmsman turned away from me at the last moment causing his stern to brush very slightly against mine. There was only a tiny nick on my boat but it revealed some dubious looking wood and the following Spring I rebuilt the transom.

ADVICE

I once had a high school art teacher who told the class that every seascape or picture showing water should have land in the lower foreground, otherwise the water would appear to be running out of the picture.

One ought to be skeptical about rules and advice. Examine them and see if they make sense, but follow them only in agreement.

The same teacher on another occasion quoted a famous illustrator as saying, "Never cut a tugboat in half." I never did know what that meant.

INDEX TO THE BOATS

*Includes 20' bowsprit

Name	Page(s)	Designer	Builder	L.O.A.	Year Built
SOUFFLE	118	Wm. H. Tripp	built in Holland	37'10"	1961
Star Class	114, 115	Francis Sweisguth (after designs by William Gardner)		22'7½"	1911
STARSAL	47	Sparkman & Stephens	John Trumpy & Sons,	40'	1950
STORMSVALA	59	F. A. Fenger	E. Nordbjaerg, Denmark	48'6"	1938
STORMY WEATHER	51	Sparkman & Stephens	Henry B. Nevins, Inc.	53'11"	1934
Super Sprite Class	16	Robert Baker	O'Day Corp.	10'	
SUSAN ANN	71	John G. Alden	Harvey Gamage	43'1"	1927
SUWANEE	94	L. E. Frye	L. E. Frye	32'	1908
SYRA	59	Robert E. Derecktor	Robert E. Derecktor	55'	1962
TALARIA	71	L. Francis Herreshoff	Morse Shipbuilding	55'	1956
TAMARACK	74, 127	Alex Strickland	Alex Strickland, Newfoundland	55'	1945
TANG	36	Chas. Crosby	Crosby	24'	1910
TANNIS II	127	Scott Carter	Scott Carter	37'9"	1937
TAPPAN ZEE	172	Isaac Gavitt	Peterson Boat Works	38'	1939
Thistle Class	117	Gordon K. Douglass	Douglass & McLeod	17'	1946
THUNDERBIRD	80	(Colin Archer type)	Hull built in Norway	37'	
THUNDERHEAD	125	Philip L. Rhodes	Abeking & Rasmussen Lemwerder, Germany	48'5"	1961
TICONDEROGA	58, 152	L. Francis Herreshoff	Quincy Adams Yacht Yd.	72'	1936
TIGER	45	designer & builder unknown built at Norwalk, Conn.		27'8"	1869
TROIKA	65	Jim Brown	Built in Canada		1967
VALIANT	132	Sparkman & Stephens	Robert E. Derecktor	63'	1969–70
WANDELAAR	120	C. William Lapworth	Jensen Marine	47'9"	1967
WEATHERLY	129	Philip L. Rhodes (Modified by Rhodes & A. E. Luders, Jr. (1962)	Luders Marine	69'	1957–58
WELKIN	51	German Frers	built in Argentina	44'6"	1957
WILD GOOSE	125	Robert E. Derecktor	Robert E. Derecktor	41'	1965
WINDLASSIE	119	Charles M. Hunt	Surfliner	34'	1960
WINSOME	50	Philip L. Rhodes	Cheoy Lee, Hong Kong	40'9"	1966
Zekeboat	95	F. W. Westerson	Built in Florida	22'	1966